# Keep It
# Simple,
# SMARTYPANTS!

STOP OVERTHINKING. START ALIGNING. LIVE HAPPY.

D1502892

# I LOVE THIS BOOK!

—Josh Greenbaum, Founder & Consulting CFO, The Accounting Company

This book packs in a ton of information on how to shift your perspective to manifest a better life. If you're seeking routes for the life you want but feel it's unattainable for some reason, it provides the stepping-stones to get you there. I loved the one-sentence takeaways. I'll reread this book to help cement it into my thought process. I loved it! — Katie McDonald, COO (Echo Ridge – University of Colorado)

I've read this book over and over, and every single time I get something new out of it.

— Kym McNicholas, Emmy Award Winning Journalist

As a therapist, I thought I knew a lot about combining thoughts and feelings in important ways, but Christine's easy applications empower you to use your emotions as guidance to become a powerful creator of your own reality. Using her expertise has truly changed my life and my work in ways I could never have imagined. — Amber Cleveland Lewter, LPC Therapist and Coach

Clear, easy-to-understand, humorous, accurate and straightforward — this book is all of those things. This is a wonderful book for anyone who wants to understand their power and also relevant for people who are more smartypants-y about that kind of thing. I can't wait to read all of the other books that I know are coming as well!

— Adam Rockefeller Growald, Investor, Entrepreneur, Philanthropist

*Keep It Simple, Smartypants!* is fabulous — not to mention absolutely beautiful. I started reading and couldn't stop!

—Beth Benatti-Kennedy, MS, LMFT Leadership Coach, Author, and Speaker

I found this book really impactful and accessible, and I thoroughly enjoyed reading it — Christine provided me with readily-usable actions for day-to-day life, that I immediately applied and benefited from in tangible and direct ways. —Kate Ayala, Chief Program Officer

# I'm so impressed.

I love the message, and even better — the way Christine got it across. She kept it simple, straightforward and fun. She's the bomb. —Jennifer Copeland, Commercial Account Manager

This book is a perfect blend of deep understanding of Law of Attraction and fun, upbeat commentary on tuning in to your soul. Having worked with Christine for years, some of the deep Law of Attraction topics we talked about early-on were a lot to wrap my mind around, but this book dives deep enough without losing the reader. **If you're seeking higher meaning, the remedy to life's problems, or to disrupt current routines and habits, this is for you.** Any problem you have is minuscule in comparison to the power you have within. Most of the mantras in this book, I still use to this day. I'm excited to read it again. —Zach Hoesly, Author and On-Air Personality

This is a well-done, incredibly positive, easy-to-understand, and informative book that includes steps that are easy to follow. Within these pages are constant reminders that I can use to improve the quality of my life and I can't wait to exercise the steps more frequently. I loved it and kept wanting more!

—Ronell Martz, Advertising Executive, *Lehigh Valley Style*

This book is very readable, with catchy, humorous, and relatable messages and action items that make it easy to put its powerful lessons into practice.

—Lisa VanderVeen, Director of Admissions, The Willow School

I want everyone I know to have their own copy of this book. It really lives up to its title in that it is such sage advice, so simply stated. It packs a punch and gets right to the point which makes it so much easier to read and really "get," and it's so inclusive, crossing any barriers of gender, age, race, religion etc. **It is great for anyone who wants to empower themselves and create the life they desire** and can draw inspiration from, no matter where they are in their lives.

—Gabriela Effron, Real Estate Broker and General Contractor, Los Angeles, CA

ISBN 978-1-7346634-0-2

Edited by Rachel Allen, Bolt from the Blue Copywriting
Designed by Sutton Long

christinemeyercoaching.com
christine@christinemeyercoaching.com
facebook.com/christinemeyercoaching
instagram.com/christinemeyercoaching

# Part 1

# Part 2

# The point of this book

is to confirm your power to you. It is to highlight and amplify what's right and good about you rather than highlight what's wrong, broken and needs to be fixed about you. (How refreshing, right?)

You were born with a perfect connection to your soul, with the power to experience any life you want, and a fool-proof compass directing you towards your connection, and towards the desires that you identify and discover as you live your life. Nothing can take that away from you. (Seriously, nothing in this universe can make you anything less than what you are, and what you are is astonishingly powerful.)

The point of this book is for you to live a good-feeling life and to have what you want, but first, to live a good-feeling life and then to have what you want. The big event of your life is the accomplishment of your blended-ness with your soul, on-your-way-to your goals, desires and manifested results. Therefore, this book is written to deepen your understanding of who-you-really-are, how powerful you are, and how to make sense of your role in this universe that you operate in.

When you resonate with who you really are, you discover your own path to your own answers. Everyone has guidance within them, and this book will help you tune to that.

I won't tell you what to do, I'll encourage you toward, and show you ways how, to tune in-to your own wisdom and knowing. What I know for sure is that every one of us has a deeper knowing that will resonate with the words on these pages. My intention is to resonate with something you know deeply about yourself — not to upset or contradict other beliefs. What you've believed so far, has worked. I'm here to speak to your soul — your innate knowing. This book is about an approach to life that has the potential to change your life.

Within these pages you'll find information that can serve you for the rest of your lifetime.

It's about a new approach to being; it's about the mastery of your own life, while also knowing that mastery is never done. It's about establishing new foundations, some of which you might be aware of, and others you might not. If you base and build your life upon false foundations or premises, the answers only serve to build upon those false premises.

**The foundations presented in this book** are consistent and true. As you apply them to create and build your life upon, you'll show yourself that nothing is random, the universe responds to you, and that you truly are a powerful being.

It is my desire to inspire and call you to the knowing and wisdom that you have within you, and for you to know how to connect to that knowing. It is my desire for you to follow your path and do what's right for you, even if (or when), it's different from the information you're receiving from family, friends or strangers — perhaps "experts" — what you're seeing on social media, reading in a book (even this book) or hearing on podcasts.

# I want you to trust yourself, your intuition, your guidance, and your knowing.

By reading this book, you'll understand how to start doing that.

There isn't a wrong way or a right way to approach your life, but there are principles that you can integrate that will assist you in living and loving *your* right life.

Consider this book a reminder of what you already inherently know. A refresher course in the power of yourself, your connection, and your soul. And above all, a calling into a life where you joyfully, playfully, fully LIVE.

# PART ONE

You
need to
know
three
things:

# FOUNDATION 1:

## You have a soul.

We are all energy beings, which means we're energy in motion. I'm not talking about some way-out-there concept, I'm talking about physics. Everything in the universe is either matter or energy, or a blend of both, including you.

You are matter and you are also energy. Same thing, different form, still one. Energy is matter, matter is energy.

You're not only physical in the you-being-you sense, but you're also energy. There's an aspect or part of you that you and others (usually) can't see, but exists. Some people call it your soul, your aura, non-physical, or all kinds of other things. Regardless of how you refer to it, it's energy. That's the simplest way to think about it.

You also happen to be incredibly good at interpreting and translating that energy. In fact, you do it so naturally and constantly, you might not be aware that that's what you're doing. Sight, sound, touch, and smell all involve an exchange of energy on a molecular and cellular level; everything vibrates (or has a resonance/frequency) which you interpret with your senses into something you can understand. This energy interpretation can also take the form of feelings — just as you translate vibrations into sounds, your spirit conveys vibrations or resonances that you interpret into emotions.

Every particle in the universe speaks the language of energy, broadcasting its own frequency or mix of frequencies out into the universe which are being responded to. You do it. Your dog does it. Your houseplants do it. The cells of your body do it. They're all streams of energy, emitting frequency, all tiny offshoots of the big, universal stream, manifested into various forms.

# One of which just happens to be you.

# This non-physical stream of energy is you, and you are it.

Part of the big stream of consciousness chose to manifest as you, and continues to flow to you, through you and as you. The you-part-of-you that's here representing as, "the human," is the one that decides how you want to direct that energy.

# So, to recap: you're a mix of matter and energy.

The energy part is a "rivulet," if you will, of the big, universal stream of energy, manifested in the form of you.

You get to decide how you want to direct your particular energy — you're not a puppet on a universal string, you're the channel and steward of the stream you've got. In fact, you, my friend, agreed with your soul to be born.

SPLAT.

You and your soul agreed that you would have an infinite relationship with each other, co-creating forever. When you were still only in energy/soul form, you experienced "oneness" in the sense that you didn't experience any discord or dissonance or difference in your being.

Once you were born, there was a potential for you to feel a "separateness" from your soul, but you and your soul agreed that while you might experience the sensation of that, or perceive it as that, you would never actually be separated. Your soul said, "Dude, I've got your back. Never leaving ya. Nope. Never. Nada. Not gonna happen. We're in this together. You go and have fun, explore, discover, create, make, do, be, and I'll always let you know I'm right there with you, having fun, exploring, discovering, creating, making and doing through you, with you, and because of you."

Your soul holds steady on its end, radiating a perfect knowing of who you are: this magnificent creator who was born to explore. It never loses sight of your birth-given worthiness and value. You never have to prove anything to it, and you certainly never have to earn its love, appreciation, or validation. It thinks you're the bomb, and you're never going to talk it out of that.

# It knows you can create, have, do, or be anything that your little heart desires once you're on planet Earth, and you're never going to dissuade it from knowing that either.

But once you go exploring on Earth, you might forget; in fact, you're likely to forget, all of this that you knew when you were only a soul.

You will
forget.
You are
never
**forgotten.**

**You see,** you got surrounded by other humans who've also forgotten, who were also told bullshit stories, who thought they too were here as "only" humans to prove something to some entity they can't see but who "holds all the cards" and while that energy exists (it's the same one we're talking about here), there's been a lot of screwed-up, messed-up versions of who and what that IS, that people believe without question.

And so, while you're human, (and a good one at that), you're going to come across beliefs that are already quite established, beliefs that look true not only because so many people believe them, but also because there will be evidence of those truths. You'll also come across lots of different opinions, you'll play with some people and not want to play with others. You'll want stuff, and probably lots of stuff.

You can't stop **wanting.** Your wanting **expands you** and expands **the universe.**

There are those who believe that wanting is bad, wrong or selfish — that you shouldn't want. What they (and you) might not have understood before, is that wanting is part of how this whole universe — and you — expands and evolves, so go ahead, want all you want. The other thing that is misunderstood about wanting, is that people often believe that wanting feels like yearning, or "missing," when in fact, "wanting," or desire, in its most aligned form feels like satisfaction, anticipation, eagerness, and/or positive expectation, which is far from "yearning" or lackful. You might also hear that you can't have what you want — which is another false premise from which humans operate.

No matter what you've heard and no matter what you've come to believe, just know that...

# You and your soul are up to bigger things.

The two of you are here, on the leading edge, creating, leading us all because you're here on Earth. Your soul is going to stay in the non-physical realm, but the physical you and your soul are never going to be truly separated. Whatever you think about, your soul has an opinion, which is actually your opinion — though you may have forgotten that perspective. Your soul will constantly remind you of that perspective, through how you feel.

Which leads us to Foundation 2...

# Found

Your emotions are

# ation 2:

## incredibly important.

( But probably not
for the reasons
you might think. )

# OK recap:

You have a soul.

You and that soul experienced oneness.

Then you decided to be born into matter. (Again, splat.)

And you mostly forgot about the soul thing. Which led you to experience a feeling of separation, (yet you never stopped wanting that connection).

But your soul didn't go anywhere. It's still right there-here-there with you. And it's constantly communicating with you through your emotions.

You can feel oneness and connection with your soul right here and now.

# Your feelings are EVERYTHING

They're a direct line to your soul and the perfect feedback on how aligned your perspective is with it — how you're managing your connection.

When you feel happy, that's an indicator that your current perspective is resonating and connecting with the perspective of your soul — which means your frequencies are similar. Any range of feelings, from peacefulness, contentment, pleasure, satisfaction, excitement, joy, exhilaration — those are all perspectives that are aligned with your soul perspective.

Similarly, when you feel bad, that's simply an indicator of a gap or a dis-connection between your current perspective about something and your soul's perspective about the same thing. That's all. The gap is just a gap. It doesn't mean that the condition or circumstance is bad, it doesn't mean you're bad, and it doesn't mean that anything is "wrong" — it simply means there's a gap. A dis-connection.

We're taught to think that having a bad feeling indicates that some "thing," person or circumstance is bad, and is the cause of you feeling bad, when in fact, it's just dissonance or dis-connection with your soul. We're also taught that feeling "good" means that some "thing," person or circumstance is good, and is the cause of you feeling good, when it's just resonance and connection with your soul.

Let me repeat it again, because it's really important, and it's completely opposite to what most of us are taught:

# Your feelings have almost nothing to do with your conditions or with other people. (Say what?!?!)

Feelings are simply resonance (connection) or dissonance (dis-connection) with your soul. Not indicators of good/bad, right/wrong, or better/worse. They have everything to do with your relationship between you and your soul. Everything.

But most peo

VARDS.

ple get this all

BACKW

**People believe in their emotions** as face value evidence of something going wrong or something going right. They believe that they are imposed upon you from external circumstances, or by other people, when actually, the way you feel about something is about you the thinker, you the feeler and you the interpreter of your circumstances.

You must understand that your emotions come from your resonance or dissonance with your soul, before you can understand what they mean.

"Good-feeling" emotions are good and they feel good, not because they're "better," but because they are an indicator that you're in alignment (resonance) with your soul's perspective. The good feeling comes from the resonance and is also informative of the resonance.

"Bad-feeling" emotions are good too, because they're also information about your perspective and how closely it's aligned or not, with your soul's perspective.

The point is, you are the perceiver, the thinker, the interpreter and the feeler, and you have a direct line to your soul, which is always communicating with you in frequencies that you translate as feelings. Those emotions let you know how closely your vibe/your frequency is resonating with, or not resonating with, your soul/your "oneness." And since you are the perceiver, the thinker, the interpreter and the feeler, how you feel is all about you and your relationship with your soul, which puts you — always in charge of affecting how you feel, which also means you can change how you feel and nothing external needs to change for you to feel differently.

# It starts from within.

Your feelings are indicators, like the signals in your vehicle. Nothing more, nothing less — and if you buy into the misunderstanding that there's anything more or less going on, you can lead a whole life based on false premises by misinterpreting what your emotions really mean and indicate.

When you believe your feelings are about things or people external, you conclude things like:

"My partner didn't do X for me, which means that he doesn't love me. That feels bad, and my bad feeling means either he needs to change, or I need to leave the relationship to be happy."

*Or,* "My partner does X for me in this way, and Y for me that way, and therefore, because of what she does, I feel special."

"My job makes me unhappy. It's responsible for these bad feelings, and I don't want those feelings, so I have to control the circumstances and somehow change the conditions, or just accept that I'm going to remain unhappy if things stay the same or if I fail to control the conditions."

*Or,* "My job is amazing, it makes me happy, and I'm afraid to lose it, because if I do, I will feel bad because the thing that I believe is the reason for my happiness, will be gone."

"My parents messed me up. It's their fault. I was born in the wrong house, born to the wrong people, and in the wrong century. Now I just have to live with the damage they imposed on me and I'm going to feel this way about them and about myself for the rest of my miserable life."

*Or,* "My mom/my friend has always been there for me. I've always turned to her for advice and support. Without her, I don't know what to do. I need her to feel secure. She is the one that makes me feel this way."

"My life is hard. Bad things happen to me. More bad things are going to keep happening to me. I mess things up. I was born this way. Nothing goes right. I can't do anything to change it, things are just the way they are. And — maybe I even deserve it, because I'm bad/alone/worthless/(insert here your misunderstanding of choice)." You conclude that because you feel bad, you and your life must be bad.

*Or,* "My life is so good, and it's because of all of the good stuff that I feel good. If I didn't have the good stuff, I wouldn't feel so good."

But here's the truth: no one and no thing is in charge of how you feel. You're the only one in charge of that.

That story about how if your mother-in-law would stop meddling in your stuff, you'd feel so much better? Well, you might be happier if she stopped meddling, but you don't have to wait until she stops meddling to feel better.

That story about how if your friend/significant other/parents/family/society/community supported you, you'd feel less alone and isolated? Once again, you might feel all warm and fuzzy if those people supported you, but you don't have to wait for them to do that, to feel supported and loved.

The story about how you need your spouse to make you feel valued, respected, or heard? Feeling that within yourself is the key to allowing that from another. It's not about him or her.

The story that it's your spouse, or some other person that's the one who makes you feel loved and adored? That's also not about them. It's about you and your focus.

All the stories about all the things and all the people — like, you need to have more money before you feel abundant, get rid of your a-hole boss to feel appreciated, have your co-workers change their personalities before you cease being annoyed, or change your job, your house, your wife, your life before you feel purpose, passion or alive. All of the stories about all of the things that make you feel like it's not you who makes you feel — all of them feel true and all of them make you feel powerless because either you need or want things, conditions, circumstances or people to change so that you can feel better, or, you assign your feelings as coming "from" them — as in, they are the "cause" of them, which means if they don't keep doing what they're doing, or if they leave, or things change, you'll not have the capacity to feel this way (the way that you feel because of the person, place, thing, condition you believe is the reason for how you feel).

While your stories feel true to you, they're false in the sense that you have more power and ability to affect your experience of those experiences than you might know. If you believe that anything or anyone makes you feel any way, you've got yourself hooked in to a false premise of what your feelings mean and where they come from.

# Unhook yourself.

**Any story that you tell** about anything that "makes you feel" any kind of way, is false — because it's not the person, it's not the thing, it's not an event, it's not the conditions, it's not the circumstances, it's not the "reality" of anything that makes you feel anything. It's your perspective of it, your interpretation of it, your meaning of it that makes you feel how you feel, and how your perspective aligns, or aligns not-so-much with your soul's perspective and opinion, that IS what "makes you feel" how you feel.

It's not the stuff or the people you've been blaming, it's your perspective and opinion(s) of the stuff and the people you've been blaming that either allows your oneness and connection with your soul (to a greater or lesser extent) or disallows (dis-connects) your oneness with your soul (to a greater or lesser extent).

Recognize that blame or assignment for how you feel runs mostly unchecked. Other scenes you might set where you do that like a runaway train include and are not limited to — the government and how it "makes you feel," climate changes, how your kid behaves or doesn't, what your neighbor is doing, and what your body is or isn't doing. From global "issues" to in-house and up-close-and-personal-to-you issues, if you believe that it's because of those conditions, things, and/or those people that you feel how you feel, you're hooked in to some false premise.

Even the story about how you need to get your shit together, explore the depths of your emotions and neuroses, search for validation and justification of them so you can somehow become a "better" person, so that you can eventually feel better? Oh-so-false and hooked in to the false premise.

Nobody, no thing, makes you feel any kind of way — good or bad.

Nobody, no thing, does anything to you.

And there's nothing wrong with you.

You don't have to go down any kind of rabbit hole to understand WHY you feel bad. That's a sure road to making up more bullshit stories based on more bullshit premises. All you're going to find down the rabbit hole are more rabbits. (We all know how those cute fluffy things multiply).

Because —
*brace yourself*
— it's all you.

# FOUNDATION

# Reality doesn't happen

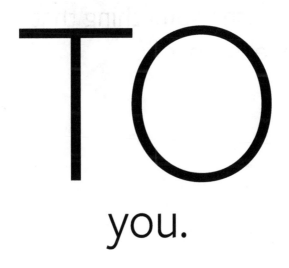

TO

you.

It happens from you.

The idea that reality happens TO you is another false premise that many people believe. That belief perpetuates another belief which is that, "life is random," that things happen randomly, by chance, by luck (or lack thereof), or for some "reason" decided by some universal force or "God."

Powerless.

More control isn't what you need.

More imaginary bubbles around your "field" isn't what you need more of, either.

# "Luck" isn't something that "happens" to you.

Is life just truly random?

Nope.

It's all you, cupcake.

Popular logic goes, "When things go well, it's because I control, ummm, I mean — manage them."

But if one thing goes wrong, you perceive that your control is flawed and its existence is at risk, so now you have to try harder and control more. Typically that looks like micromanaging, whining, bullying, stressing, coercing, manipulation — that sort of thing.

(Isn't that exhausting? I know I'm exhausted just thinking about it.)

"But what's the alternative?" you ask.

It's giving up the idea that you need to (or can) control everything, and start understanding that you create everything.

Everything comes FROM you, not at you.

Everything is FOR you, not against you.

# The essence of that which you think often, and the essence of that which you feel consistently, becomes your reality.

As noted, how you feel lets you know your proximity to your soul's frequency — more resonance or dissonance with what your soul knows, and feels about you, and/or about what you're thinking about. Your soul has an opinion and a perspective about all things that you think about. Your soul also knows everything that your little heart desires and becomes the frequency of your desires. So when you think a thought and have a feeling response to it, that's information for you.

If you feel good/if what you're thinking about and the emotional feedback you're receiving feels good, you're on-track, or in resonance with your soul. This also means you're in-this-moment resonating with your desires and what you want. If you feel "bad"/if what you're thinking about and how you're thinking about it provides emotional feedback that doesn't feel good to you, that's information for you that lets you know that in-this-moment, you're opposing that desire (to a greater or lesser degree, depending on how crappy you feel.) This means you are thinking about the lack or absence of your desire, which indicates that you are creating dissonance between you and your soul perspective because of the way you're focusing/thinking about that thing.

Everything comes from you, not at you.
Everything is for you, not against you, and...
Your thoughts evolve into manifested matter.

Let's break that down a little more. Remember the whole physical/non-physical thing?

Frequencies manifest into feelings that you interpret, which become things you see that you then call "truths," "realities" or "facts." You can hang out on many frequencies, and you often do, depending on the thoughts you think.

Sound woo-woo? Let's make it SUPER practical.

Think about the last time you ate. You first had the feeling of hunger, and then a thought like, "Hey, I'm hungry. I'm going to eat something." At that point, nothing had happened yet. The meal was still theoretical. Then, you took the actions to make that meal happen. The vibrational/energetic/ theoretical meal manifested into an actual meal that you ate.

Same deal goes for everything else.

# Your frequencies are what the universe responds to.

It's like you're a walking, talking billboard ad of energy. Your thoughts, if thought long enough, frequently enough, or consistently enough, become. Which means — they manifest. Between the thoughts thought long enough and what you'd call "the manifestation" are other "manifestations." Those are the feelings you feel, more thoughts, ideas, experiences, going places, seeing and hearing things, having conversations, changing jobs, etc. The first manifestation that follows a thought though, is always a feeling.

Frequencies

thoughts.

feelings

things.

ALWAYS.

# Which means that it's all you.

Which, at first, might sound like some kind of throat-gripping, sweat-enhancing, backed-into-a-corner blame. "What do you mean, I'm the one doing these things to myself?!," you shout as your hands flail about.

Yeah, I know, but stick with me. This knowledge puts you in the driver's seat that you've always been in, but now you know it. This is a good thing. Your thoughts are like magnets, inviting equivalent experiential matches towards them. The essence of that which you think about consistently becomes, manifests, and IS your life.

# You're

doing the creating.

# You're

doing the feeling.

# You're

doing the attracting.

# You

think it into being.

**And here's the awesome part:** you're constantly getting emotional, and visible, and tangible feedback on what your vibe/your frequency is, by what's going on around you.

Your life is showing you all the time what you think and how you feel. So if what's playing out in your life feels crappy, you've been feeling crappy and thinking crappy-feeling thoughts. If what's playing out in your life feels good, you've been feeling good and thinking good-feeling thoughts. If you're getting a little bit (or a lot) of crap, and a little bit (or a lot) of good, that lets you know your feelings and thoughts are all over the place in the vibe department. Your thoughts create your life, and your feelings inform you what you're in the process of creating. It's right there for you to witness, and you're right there doing it all.

Which means that if you're the one doing it, you can change it. If it was someone or something else doing it, you'd have to try to control it, change it, injure it, lock it up, clone it, preserve it, or kick it to the curb. Let's not do any of that.

If you assign yourself the credit for your thoughts that lead to the emotions that lead to the impulses, that lead to the actions that lead to the results — whether those results are wanted or not, you empower yourself, because now you know you're in charge. It's not random, it never was. It's not being "done to you," it never was. Assigning the credit anywhere else, feels powerless.

# The universe *does* revolve around you. (Your parents were wrong when they said it doesn't).

It's all
you.

Take the
credit.

We now get to one of the really fun ones — the question of why bad things happen, if this is true that you get to take the credit for it all. The good, the bad, the ugly.

"Why would I manifest bad stuff? This is total bullshit, Christine!"

This is just a perfect example of the law of attraction. Thoughts attract, they do not "assert." You don't (for the most part) purposely manifest anything to hurt yourself or purposely attract things you don't want. Mostly, that's done through oblivion or misunderstanding. If you've been thinking and feeling and thinking and feeling and thinking and feeling, and didn't know that you attract the essence of your thoughts; if you were confused about what your feelings mean; if you were unaware of, or ignoring, how you feel altogether, it's quite easy to understand how you'd blunder into something you unknowingly or unintentionally created, is it not? The fact that you create something you don't want is just as powerful as creating something you do want. The essence of what you think and how you feel manifests if you continue to re-introduce it. Remember, frequencies -> thoughts -> feelings -> things.

If you feel unworthy, then over time as you continue to feel that way, things would happen in your life, pointing to how you're already feeling.

If you feel like things happen randomly, then things in your life would unfold, perfectly matching the essence of your feeling of being "blindsided."

When you hang around a frequency and vibration long enough, or if you keep reintroducing it, you rendezvous with manifestations that match the vibe(s) that are active in you, which of course helps you affirm that feeling even more — which also makes the feeling even "truer" to you, and the belief even stronger. (You now have "evidence.") This leads you to believe it more, which leads you to attract it more (because you keep vibing it and therefore your vibe matches it) which leads you to believe it more, which leads you to attract more of it. All of it a perpetual self-fulfilling prophecy of beliefs and affirmation of your power to create your reality.

If you look at your life, you can often spot patterns playing themselves out over and over again in just this way.

# The only thing that ever works "against" you

is your own vibe (which is comprised of the thoughts, beliefs and expectations that you have). It's only the way you're flowing energy.

Is how you're flowing energy opposing or harmonizing with your desire? One way to know how you're flowing energy is by paying attention to how you feel. Another way is by paying attention to what you say. Do your "buts" follow closely behind your statements of desire? Pay attention to what you say and let what you say reveal the clues that are there. You might "but," complain, doubt, justify, or demand your way to what you want, but it'll be as effective and difficult as trying to drive down the highway while you've got your foot on the brake pedal. Try it, you'll get the concept really quickly. Another way to know how you're flowing energy is to take a look around your life and see what's manifesting. Do you like it much, or do you like it not-so-much? It's a clue. If you like it, keep vibing how you're vibing. If you don't, there are some adjustments you can make to your vibe, which means to your mood and attitude (which is composed of your thoughts, beliefs and expectations). The good news is, the adjustments to be made are yours to make.

Everything revolves around you and your vibe. You're the attractor. How you feel, think, and perceive becomes — you're constantly surrounding yourself with evidence of that because your life is evidence of that.

If you want things to be easier or better, don't deny the struggle, but don't keep talking about it either. Talking more about it keeps you matching up with it because that's where your attention is and therefore your vibe is. And again, it's you — not "them," not "that thing," not "the system."

If you take ownership of your creation, and claim your role and your point of rendezvous within it — not in a self-blame-focused way, but simply in an acceptance of your power way — then you can free yourself from feeling like you're at the mercy of anything external, and you can shift your feelings, which is the most powerful and productive way to also shift your circumstances.

If you believe that everything and everyone around you has to change before you can feel differently, you better strap yourself in for a really long and unpleasant ride.

So, how long do you want to keep telling those stories?

If you like feeling how you've been feeling and want to experience similar things of similar vibes, keep at it! You're a powerful creator, you can keep creating everything around you, just like you've been doing.

You can take your past with you or you can make a different choice. Keep telling that story if you want to keep living it. Tell it less or tell it not at all, and instead, substitute other stories. If you *want* something different, you have to change your focus, change your stories, and adapt to a different and more empowered state of being.

To be extremely clear, this is not about saying that bad things haven't happened to you. What it IS saying is that you have the freedom to determine your perspective of those things by taking ownership of those events and your role in them. You can choose to see yourself as a victim, or as someone who is so incredibly powerful that you co-created and expanded yourself and the whole universe as a result of your experience.

# Remember that "that feels bad" doesn't have to turn into "this is bad (and only bad)" or "I am bad."

This helps you get back in touch with your soul perspective, which is a place of immense power.

You have the freedom to take you and your past with you, and you have the freedom to move toward your future. It's always up to you.

You get to live your life from a place of simple and total empowerment, because there's nothing external that's in charge of you and how you think, feel, and therefore create.

You can choose to believe that contrary to life happening TO you, everything is instead, always working out FOR you.

There is no downside to believing that things are always working out for you.

Worst case scenario? You live as though things are always working out for you (even if you don't 100% believe it just yet), and start attracting things that confirm that belief.

If you actively accept that what happens to you comes from you, therefore accepting that you do have total control, and as you decide to take credit for all things that involve you — including your responses, then your life in all its "randomness" becomes stable. Solid. Sure. The more you direct your thoughts and feelings intentionally, it becomes fun. Joyous. Rewarding. You start feeling empowered, knowing you have an open sandbox to play in, to create whatever you want. You no longer seek to control from the outside-in, because you now understand the control has always been from the inside-out through your thoughts and feelings.

These shifts don't happen overnight. They happen gradually.

Your first step toward that, is deciding that feeling good matters, and that it matters enough that you're going to consciously choose thoughts that feel better and enhance your connection, rather than thoughts that feel worse and diminish your connection. When you choose to feel better, little by little, about all things, all things change to the theme and essence of your thoughts.

# You begin to see the magnificent order at play.

The earth spins in its orbit.
The sun rises and sets.
The tides go in and out.
There's an overall balance to the planet.
The planets are in proximity to each other.
Your blood flows. Your heart pumps.
There are things in place already establishing wellbeing.

# There's magnificent order in the universe.

There's magnificent order in you being you, and in you being the creator and attractor of your life.

There's magnificent order in the sense that it's always fair. Your resonance is always being responded to, your "advertisement" is always being answered. Every vibrating being is always being met with perfect matches to its own frequencies. There's nothing of a mismatch in that plan, order, or setup.

Everything is always a perfect vibrational fit, whether you understand the fit or not.

There's magnificent order in the way things play out, because equivalent vibes harmonize with each other, always. There are no exceptions to this order. It applies to everyone and to all things.

There's a certainty that you can come to know, feel and expect in that order — a knowingness of its constancy, because you can see how it's always demonstrating itself to you.

Even the things you see as "going wrong" are actually in perfect order. Because it's not random, and it's not out of place. It may not be what you want, but it's inevitably, irrevocably happening in response to your vibrational advertisement. There's always an essence that's a perfect match for that event, circumstance, or feeling. There is only perfect synchronicity with your vibration.

There
are no
mistakes.

As you vibrate, you attract. And so, what better way to know what you're vibrating than to attract something tangible? It's a physical, hold-it-in-your-hands demonstration of what you've been vibrating, what your thoughts and emotions have been.

There's always a direct correlation between your emotions and thoughts and what's happening in your life. If you haven't been paying attention to them, then you can experience things that feel "bad" or "random," but even then, those experiences are clarifying. In experiencing what you don't want, you're learning ever-more-clearly what you do want, amplifying the vibration of that desire with your soul, which has never been confused about the desire.

# From your soul's perspective, there's never a situation that's wrong, and never one that can't be improved.

There's never a situation that's doomed, or a challenge that can't be generative. Why? Because your soul doesn't see any of those things as problems. If you break something or want something, you may see that as a problem. But your soul sees it as an opportunity to fulfill your desires, find solutions, welcome in better ideas that might otherwise have never come about, without the opportunity presented in that problem. From your soul's perspective, it's not "Oh, that's bad" it's "Oh good! Something to want! What's next?!?"

From the tiniest inconveniences to the biggest problems of your life...

Things are always working out for you.

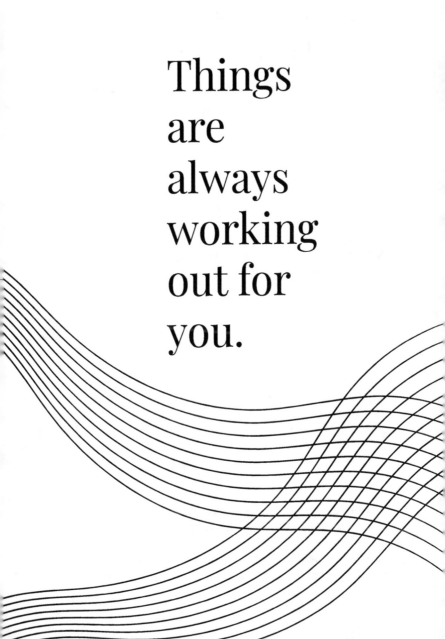

# Your success is inevitable — your joy, wellbeing, abundance, and thriving in all ways. You just have to let it in.

You can have what you want.

When people hear that, they tend to think one of two things: that, "I can have it all now, and I want it all now," or, "This is total bullshit."

"Christine, you say I can have what I want? Great! I'll take a six pack and a speedboat, a big TV and a perfect marriage, and amazing hair. Oh, and while you're at it, how about we throw in several million dollars and world peace too?"

Great! You can have that. And guess what — when you get it, you'll want more. And even in getting it, you will experience contrast and clarification. You get the TV and realize that actually what you want is more time with your spouse. Or a bigger TV. Or actually, to feel wealthy.

Everything you want is for the desire and journey and flow of energy towards it more than the having of it. The marriage of the energy of your desire and the joy of the energy of the fulfillment of it. This doesn't mean that you can't and won't enjoy having it when you get it. But that's not the end-all be-all. Your soul is interested in the experience. In the flow. In the movement of the energy. And so are you.

There's nothing your soul enjoys more than an ever-growing list of desires, because that's the way you expand your possibilities, and the universe. When you want something, you don't just expand yourself and your own parameters, you expand the whole universe. Your desires expand the possibilities for everyone, and everything else.

In case the thought of cosmic responsibility is freaking you out — we can also look at this on the individual level, and see how this frees you from the trap of "I'll be happy when..."

"I'll be happy when I have $10,000 (or more) in savings."

"I'll be happy when I have a relationship."

"I'll be happy when my partner stops leaving their clothes on the floor."

"I'll be happy when my dad stops drinking."

"I'll be happy when my kid grows up."

"I'll be happy when I lose 2/10/50/100 pounds."

"I'll be happy when women are more empowered, oppression doesn't exist, racism is extinct and when global warming, world hunger, and the government are no longer an issue."

This conditional statement of "I'll feel X when Y happens" is a universal human thought-trap.

We all fall into it. You want what you want because you think that having it, holding it, living in it, driving it, playing with it, licking it, kissing it, is going to make you happy (or rich, powerful, fulfilled, satisfied, revered, etc). You can spend your whole life chasing that happy, assigning it to others, and running away from feelings of sadness/discontentment/whatever other emotion you're trying to avoid.

But as you now know, when you're feeling any "bad" feelings of some sort, you've got to stop looking at anything external and look at yourself. The same applies for your "happy." It doesn't come from things external.

You will be happy when YOU decide to be happy, and steadily think thoughts that feel happy. It's that simple. You don't get to happy by thinking thoughts that feel crappy.

**So, to recap.** It's all you. You and your soul, partners in eternity, co-creating and playing with your desires and the joy of their fulfillment forever.

You're constantly in conversation with your soul, though the communication isn't always something you can put into words. It's your emotions. "Good" feeling emotions are an indicator of your connection, that your perspective is aligned with that of your soul's. "Bad" feeling emotions are a signal that you're less plugged in, less aligned, and less connected with your soul. Nothing more, nothing less.

You've been taught to see your emotions as something very different though: you've been taught that they're indicators of an external reality. That someone or something does something "to" you and "makes" you feel a certain way.

The truth is, reality doesn't happen to you, you create your experience of it. When you assign yourself total credit for your life, you are free. You're no longer at the mercy or control of anyone or anything, because YOU decide how you feel, and what you're going to rendezvous with. You begin to see the magnificent order in life, and how everything is always working out for you. Which means that the only question now is ...

# What
are you going to do with
# that?

Practice
awareness.

———

Own your
vibe.

———

Find the next
best feeling.

———

**Keep
doing that.**

# part 2

Applying
the
knowing
to the
doing.

# So, you're raring to go. Yay! Let's do this.

The universe is your oyster! So hustle hustle hustle and go get it. Set yourself up with an affirmation or two and let's manifest the shit out of this!

Not so fast there, cupcake. You can't "do" your way into this. At least, not without understanding and tending to the energy/the connection piece first. All that stuff we talked about with your soul, your emotions, and you being in control of your reality still matters — which means that you have to look at your connection/your alignment first.

You can get to where you want to go any way you want to. If you want to chant mantras for 10 years, fold 10,000 origami cranes, and climb the highest mountain to prove your devotion to your connection, go for it. But it can be simpler than that. If you begin from the premise that connection is your birth-given intention and "right," that you have emotional feedback which lets you know how you're managing that connection, that you can keep choosing your connection by allowing your emotions to guide you as you steer them in the direction of your connection, then why put yourself through all the work?

To put it another way, you can get down the road regardless, but doing it with effort and action alone is like trekking cross country with a heavy load on your back, worn out shoes and no food, no bed and no map. Doing it aligned, or at the very least leaning in the direction of your connection, is like going cross-country, having posh accommodations (including comfy pillows), comfy beds, your luggage taken-care-of, all the delicious food and drinks you want, with a GPS you've never seen the likes-of.

Which means that you need to focus far more on your way of being.

Here's the thing: there are two big false premises about what creates change.

False premise 1:

# You have to try hard.

# Many people believe that you have to try really hard to make changes (i.e., "struggle" and "push").

Well, you can if you want to.

But trying. And hard. Struggle. And pushing. Does any part of that feel good?

You tell me.

Think about how it feels when you're trying hard at something. Perhaps there is a part of it that feels good, and that's more than likely, focus. Focus can feel good. Typically when you're trying hard, you're also struggling, and often "pushing" or trying to force something into place or into happening. If you like it, keep it up — maybe that's your style, but if it's not really how you want to keep approaching your life and you'd like to proceed differently, read on.

Action in combination with trying hard, struggling, and pushing are not what "get things done" or what delivers the results you want. Trying hard, struggling and pushing, point to resistance. Focusing on resistant thoughts, doing stuff that feels hard, struggling or that feels like you're pushing amplifies the resistance. It makes you a match to more struggle and gives you a rougher ride than needed. If you stay at it, you can disallow indefinitely the preferred results you're going for — while you feel like crap on-the-way to more crappy stuff. Sounds good, doesn't it? I didn't think so. (Again, it's all you.)

All it takes is for you to be aligned with your desire vs. opposing your desire, 51% more of the time. It takes the scale to be tipped just a little more on the side of alignment (less resistant) rather than not-alignment (more resistant). For example, it's as simple as you feeling hopeful (or better) 51% of the time vs. feeling frustrated, impatient, doubtful, discouraged or worse 51% of the time.

Accept that you're likely to put some resistance in the way some of the time, simply because that's part of you being human. Your soul will never stop guiding you around it though (without judgment). Your soul does not care if you have resistance. Resistance doesn't mean you're doing something "wrong" or that you're "bad," faulty, weak, or incapable. Resistance affects your experience of your experience and your resistance matches you up with things that match your resistance. Resistance means you're not feeling as good along the way as you could, which also means your connection to your soul is "weaker" in those moments and things will feel harder than they need to feel.

# More resistance = things will feel harder, and be harder.

You might interpret that to mean, "It's not meant to be," "It's harder than it needs to be," "It's taking too long." It might feel like a roller coaster, emotionally and in how it's all playing out. Less resistance (more alignment) = easier, smoother, things falling into place with more flow. Resistance means resistant thoughts. Resistance means thoughts that don't match the frequency of your soul, your true knowing and/or your desires. They're the thoughts that "dis-connect" you from your oneness. Resistance is present if and when you're feeling negative emotion. Resistance is what gets in the way of allowing your full connection, and also what gets in the way of, limits or "skews" your experience and the receiving of what you want, because resistance indicates vibrational contradiction is present. Resistance is not bad. Resistance isn't something you need to avoid. Welcome it, because being aware of it lets you decide what to do about it.

You don't have
to emphasize the
struggle to be
worthy of the gain.

# IT only happens with action.

# So, how do you accomplish anything if you're not struggling?

Or pushing? Or trying really hard to make it happen? Great question, smartypants. Well, our next false premise is that you need to take action — often, and a lot of it. But this is also a misunderstanding. Action is essential, but it is only truly effective, fun, inspired and productive when it comes from your aligned and connected state of being and energy.

Humans tend to be reactors to life, often seeking the action as the solution to the "problem," taking actions to overcompensate for the results they're getting from the misalignment of their energy. They're trying to create through action rather than understanding where creation begins and mostly happens, which is first in thought. If you don't take the time (or don't care) to align and establish your connection first, you'll continue to have similar outcomes, similar approaches, or similar experiences again and again. Same patterns in relationships, same patterns in business, work, friends, money, body, everything. "Same shit, different day." Yep.

Why is that, and how is that? The results you get are a match (or reflection) of your vibe. Perfect order, remember? If the action(s) you take are "inspired" from your resistant vibe, what do you think you're perpetuating? More or less resistance? More or less of what you want, or more or less of what you don't want?

Just imagine you're pushing a ball up a slope. You can absolutely push the ball up the slope. But if you move your foot, it's going to roll back down the hill, and you're going to have to roll it back up again. If you want it to stay there you're going to have to constantly expend energy to keep it there.

But if you move the ball to a flat area (aka get your alignment sorted out first), then getting that ball where you want it to go, and keeping it there, becomes way easier.

Action
can't and
won't
compensate
for
MISALIGNMENT
(your resistance).

So whenever you want to "do" something, focus on how you're being and feeling first — focus on your connection. Your connection (your vibe/your frequency) will inspire the thoughts, the ideas and subsequently the actions will follow from the aligned flow of energy.

Your thoughts determine how you feel, which inspires your actions. Actions you take when you're feeling better than worse (more connected than less connected) are more productive, fun, far more effortless, and effective.

It's kind of like the difference between frantically shoving a bunch of food in your mouth, trying to chew it all up fast, swallow it, and discovering you've overeaten, vs. taking an appropriate bite of food, savoring it, easily chewing and swallowing it, and feeling satiated and perfectly satisfied.

The purpose of action isn't necessarily to accomplish something. The purpose of action is to move in the direction of — it's a means for your energy to flow.

The purpose of action is to celebrate an inspired thought. Action is to inspiration as a party is to planning. One is better with the other.

Whatever you want, don't just **DO** it. **BE** it and **FEEL** it.

# step one:

## Awareness

# Thinking yoga, meditations, or counting breaths?

By awareness, I mean paying attention to what you're feeling and thinking, and then making the correlation between what you're feeling and thinking, to what's happening in your life.

You're having thoughts and feeling responses to those thoughts all day long, but you're (perhaps) mostly ignoring most of those feeling responses to your thoughts. You're not paying attention to your mood and attitude all that much and if you are, you're not associating your mood with the thoughts you're thinking. Instead you're associating it with him, her, them, that, or it. Your moods and attitudes are often reactive to what you're observing, rather than choosing them on purpose.

Am I right? Probably.

This means you're unaware of the signals you're broadcasting (your vibe) and your connection or lack thereof, and thereby, tend to get "blindsided" by things that you didn't see coming — all of which perfectly match your vibe, your mood, your attitude. Remember, there's no "random."

You can't possibly pay attention to all the thoughts you're thinking (nor would you want to), but you can be more attentive to how you're feeling and care more about your mood, which you can do something about, on purpose.

Intentionally.

Instead of moving through the day like a hummingbird flitting from thought to feeling to thought to feeling, observing and reacting, observing and reacting — pay attention to how you're feeling, care about how you feel, know you're in charge and do something about the charge that is yours. What you put attention to, expands. What you focus on becomes more. So what emotions do you think you want to pay particular attention to? The ones that enhance your connection, yes. And which ones do you want to notice, (not ignore), but decide if you want to keep pointing there, highlighting, making a big deal about, dramatizing, and emphasizing?

The ones that diminish your connection, yes. All feelings are information that you can use for your benefit. All feelings are guidance for you to make a choice about what you're going to amplify and tune to. Your mood is a clue to your thoughts, observations, focus and associated feelings, informing you of your allowing or disallowing/limiting of your connection with your soul and its perspective.

Why does it matter if you're aligning and connecting with your soul's perspective? Because it feels good when you do (which is your reason for existing). When you're connected with your soul's perspective, you're also allowing your connection/your cooperation with/you become the frequency of your soul and of your desires, which means that you're in-this-moment, also not resisting or blocking what you want. You're in the flow of the energy.

Whether you're aware of your emotions or not, it's common in our culture to focus more heavily on the negative ones. "The good-feeling ones, they just feel good. These "bad-feeling" ones, we'd better sort-out, "fix," get rid-of, analyze, and form groups about them." Much unnecessary labor and attention is applied to bad-feeling feelings like "I'm concerned, I'm worried, I'm tired, I'm overworked, I feel broken, life is hard, etc."

When you pick up or repeatedly introduce negative-feeling thoughts, it's like deliberately trying to have a nightmare again and again. Why put yourself through it? And, more to the point, why would you ever expect that would get you somewhere you want to go? Is there any real good that comes out of repeatedly and purposely having a nightmare?

# So, let's practice awareness.

Start by choosing something you know feels bad every time you think about it. Something that feels like tension, sadness, irritation — something "mild" like that. (These emotions indicate you have some resistance in the mix.) Think about it, focus on it, tune to it, knowing that we're not going to stay here long.

Got it? Stay there for at least a minute, not more than two. Set a timer. Go.

How did it feel to you? Was it light and enjoyable, or did it feel like you'd picked up a boulder and dropped it on your chest? Did you start to feel worse or better the more time you hung-out in that vibe, thinking about what you were thinking about?

Now, this part is important: nothing actually, physically changed when you did this. Whatever you thought about wasn't happening right now. You thought it, and your feelings responded. Your feelings let you know that you just "dis-connected" with that thought, or with your perspective of that subject. Thought —> feeling.

Nothing changed, and yet you felt differently.

Now let's do this with a better feeling. Think about something that you know you feel good when you think about it. It could be your pet, your socks, your volleyball team, the feeling of sand between your toes, the sun rising, music you like — anything that you know feels good when you think about it.

Think, and feel. Feel and think on this subject and bask in it for at least a minute, preferably two. Set a timer. Go.

Did you feel the feeling response to your thoughts, or the subject of your thoughts? How did that feel to you? Did your heart get warm, your hands tingle? Maybe you smiled, and felt like you were right back there in that good moment, with that person or pet or thing you love? Did you feel better or worse as you focused in that way? Did you feel more connected or less connected? More harmony or more dissonance?

Again, what you were thinking about wasn't actually happening. All that changed was your focus. You purposely thought about something that felt good, that you knew would feel good when you thought about it.

You felt a different emotional response/received different emotional feedback depending on the subject of your focus and perspective of that subject.

It's important to be able to make this distinction. This is your soul communicating to you and you receiving that communication.

Cool, isn't it? Can you feel and distinguish for yourself, that this change of feeling occurred with your change of focus/thought/attention, and is totally in your control? Can you feel that direct correlation? It is independent of circumstances in that moment, but you affected your vibe and connection with what you were focusing on.

**This is incredibly simple.** It's so simple, that you might even think it's irrelevant, ineffective, and that it has to be/should be harder than this. There you go, being human again. This is the most powerful thing you can possibly do, because awareness is what allows you to do anything else. Even if you never "do" anything else, if you are aware of your emotional responses, you now have the power to choose more — to make more decisions about how you want and prefer to feel, and to make more decisions about what you choose to think about. You can consciously choose more or less connection, rather than accidentally blundering into more or less connection.

Life no longer feels "random," it's simply cause and effect.

Practicing awareness allows you to reframe your perspective with feedback from your emotions guiding you toward more or less connection, which is valuable in creating and living the life you want — no longer moving forward under false premises about what your feelings mean. It's like the difference between building a house on quicksand and building one on a solid foundation.

It's the difference between building and living in a house you don't like much (if at all) and building and living in a house you love that can endlessly please you. You now also know when you're standing in your own way by bringing resistance into the mix. If you're taking action that is from a disconnected state of being, things will feel harder. Any "success" you manage to "push" through will be limited and much less than you could experience from a more aligned and connected, therefore less resistant state of being and approach.

To be clear: the distinction here is knowing whether you're connected/ aligned or not. One isn't better or worse than the other. You don't get more stars on the chart for tuning to your connected state of being, rather than tuning to your less-than-connected version of yourself. It's knowing the difference that matters, because knowing the difference gives you the choice to pick one, or the other. To lean in one direction more (remember the 51%?), or to lean in the other direction, and know you're doing it. This is not a reason to beat yourself up. It's not a statement of your value, how worthy you are, or even how "good" or "bad" you are at this game. It's simply awareness and the ability to choose.

Because, remember, feelings are solely a way to gauge your resonance or dissonance between your current perspective and that of your soul's. There's nothing inherently wrong, bad, worse, good, or better, about them, other than some feel more pleasant while others feel more unpleasant.

While unwanted things happen, and your life will cause you to feel some "negative emotional responses" and while things happen that we label, track, analyze, and identify ourselves with, (or fear perhaps for our lifetime), it's not necessary. You don't have to keep feeling bad about anything, and while it's not wrong, you can feel better.

# What matters most is that you know the difference and you care about how you feel.

Unless you make that correlation, you're not going to care and you're not going to do anything about it. There is no judgment as to whether you are in alignment or not. There's just knowing the difference, knowing that you can choose a better feeling over a worse feeling if you want to.

# This is true

### empowerment.

# step 2:

Own
your vibe.
Own your
creations.

# Remember the premise that reality doesn't happen TO you?

This means that you can change anything. You are in total control, first in your ability to guide yourself toward more or less connection, and secondly, as you choose, your vibe adjusts, which changes how the world around you responds to you. Anything can be modified. Anything can change. You can change it. To do that, you have to own your vibe, and own your rendezvous points resulting from your vibe. Be proud of it, no matter what it is, because you're the creator of your reality. You're so powerful, you create your reality through your thoughts because they vibrate, the frequencies of which attract and become manifested "matter" either as "things" or as your experience of things, relationships, interactions, and conditions.

You have a relationship with all things you think about.

Everything that you rendezvous with is your creation. There may be others involved, but you're the owner of your points of rendezvous and how you rendezvous with it. To own it empowers you, not only to recognize the correlation of cause and effect, but also to feel empowered to make changes if you want to.

Own, the "good," the "bad" and the "ugly." Own the "lucky breaks." It isn't luck. You create that. That amazing person you met? You did that. That stunning sunrise you saw had your name on it long before you ever saw it. Your rendezvous points are yours.

Own when someone's acting in a way you don't like. Don't own their behavior, own that your vibe (which consists of your thoughts, beliefs and expectations) makes you a perfect match to that rendezvous. It's not your "fault," it's purely cause and effect. Your mother-in-law does that really annoying thing? Your frequency matched up with her for example, either because you were already annoyed, or you expect her to be annoying based on past experience, and you rendezvous with her when she's being annoying. She fulfills your vibrational request (because you ask with your vibe). She might be a really nice person and annoy no one else on the planet but you, but with you — she just can't help but be annoying because that's where your vibe is, about her.

Wherever your vibe is, you are met.

**Another example could be feeling stressed at work.** It could be a perpetual cycle of thoughts and observations, to which you feel stressed, to which your vibe is matched, to which you react by feeling more stressed, which attracts more people, work, situations etc., that match your feelings of stress. It's easy to blame others or blame the circumstances and give them the credit or blame for the "bad fortune" or "good fortune" you rendezvous with, but "those" people and "those" things are cooperating with your vibe. Perhaps you should thank them for showing you more clearly how or what you've been thinking and feeling and where you're vibing. Don't blame. Take the credit.

Ownership affirms your power and who you were born to be — as the creator of your reality. Ownership acknowledges and allows you to feel and know that you are the source of everything that happens in relationship to you and through you. You are the source. Let me repeat:

# YOU are the source.

So, when you rendezvous with something that you don't like, you can say, "I did that!"

When you rendezvous with something you do like, you can say, "I did that!"

Either way, it's something to celebrate. When you own it, you can change it.

When you decline ownership, you diminish your experience of yourself.

## To repeat:

Owning your vibe and your creations is not an invitation to beat yourself up.

It is intended to be empowering, not disempowering. It's not to be taken in the way that you did something bad, or wrong, or in some way "deserve" the unwanted things you've attracted.

It's simply a reflection of your vibe. A mirror for you to see it more clearly. If you're thinking thoughts and having emotional feedback, the essence of that will match up with a variety of things that could be more or less wanted or not wanted.

If you get up in the middle of the night and stub your toe, you didn't purposely mean to stub your toe. It's also not a "curse," you don't "deserve" it, and it's definitely not a "sign" of anything other than pointing to some "static," some resistance, some dissonance, some ever-so-slight disconnection in the form of irritation, annoyance, or even being in a hurry. Your vibe was just "off" and stubbing your toe could be enough for you to stop, pay attention, and ask yourself, "What's my mood?," "How am I feeling?" and "How do I want to feel?" Reset. Go.

This knowledge is not intended to be yet another stick to beat yourself up with. It's intended to let you throw that stick away, and simply live in the journey of connection, moving incrementally in the direction of your joy.

Everything you create is information. It's an affirmation of your power.

Downside to believing this? None. We're trained by society and others to focus more negatively than positively, and to weigh the pros and cons, plusses and minuses and to be (for the most part) more skeptical and cynical than optimistic and trusting. We're taught to be conditional, to wait for X condition to happen so that we can be relieved/happy/joyful/content etc., when it does happen, rather than being and feeling those emotions now.

# "When" is a trap.
# "Now" is powerful.

Taking this approach is a lifestyle/being change, not a "fad." It has the probability of freeing you from conditionality and externality. When you own your vibe, you're no longer at the mercy of circumstances, and you're no longer waiting for "when," or "if." The whole universe is at your disposal, just waiting to fulfill your desires, so why not be happy now, or at least lean in the direction of it? Why not anticipate more positively than more negatively? Why not feel better than worse? Why not be content with what you have, while simultaneously understanding that it's just a piece of where you're going, that this piece is relevant to where you're going, but it's not the end and things can and will improve, change, evolve and become.

Why not remember your ownership and your power?

**So, try it.** You're aware now. You can't "unknow" this knowledge. You might choose to ignore it, but you can't unknow it. Take deliberate ownership of your vibe. Take ownership of your thoughts. Take ownership of your feelings. Take ownership of your perspective. Take ownership of your results. Take full-on ownership.

Whether it's something that feels "good" or "bad," or whether it's something wanted or not, ask yourself what it might be like if you took total ownership of it. If you claimed it, took the credit, acknowledged that you created it, and gave yourself a pat on the back — all of it free of condemnation. No matter what you rendezvous with, you can celebrate your role and your power in attracting it.

See how much more satisfying that feels to you than thinking "Oh, this thing happened to me" or "Oh, this was totally out of my control." Feel into each of those beliefs, and see which one feels better to you. What feels more powerful, believing that you create (and therefore can change) your life and attract whatever you want, or believing that you're at the mercy of your circumstances and everyone around you?

You are the
# creator
of your reality.

How cool is that?!

# step three:

## Find the next best feeling.

**OK, so you've experienced and practiced awareness.** You're taking ownership of your vibe, which means you're taking ownership of your thoughts, your perspectives and how you feel and you're taking ownership of your creations. You're getting a sense (or a glimpse) of how powerful you are. With that understanding, you can now do something to create the changes you want.

"Yay! Action!!"

Well, yes, sort of. You can put the horses back in the barn for now. We don't need them just yet.

Are you ready for the huge, world-changing, magic Jedi action to take to create the world you want?

## Here it is: Find the next best feeling. Whatever that means in-that-moment, to you.

I know — earth-shattering. See why I told you to put the horses back in the barn for now?

The "doing" here, is not really "doing" in the ways you might think. It's not about taking action (not quite yet), it's about getting into alignment, tuning your vibe, and getting plugged in. Because, as you now know, your connection is your superpower. The more connected you are, the clearer you are, the better you feel, and the more inspired you are to take those actions you so eagerly want to take.

It's about tuning your frequency closer to the vibe of your soul's. It's about plugging in to that socket. It's about choosing thoughts or choosing subjects that feel better. If you're feeling really bad, then feel for a thought that feels kinda-bad or slightly better than really bad. From there, one that makes you feel just a little bad. Not worse. Then, maybe one that makes you feel neutral. Maybe generally bad rather than so specifically bad. That's it. You're right on track. It might feel a little hard at first because you've been fixated on the thing that you're feeling bad about and there's likely some momentum there, but what you're going for is a small-and-ever-so-slight shift in how you feel. Feel the relief. Feel the slight improvement.

If you're feeling good, there's always room for you to focus and feel for a thought that feels even better. Your ability to feel good, or bad, is infinite.

This is about finding a thought for the sake of how it feels. Not for the "truth" of it, the "fact" of it, the "evidence" of it, or the popularity of it, but simply for how it feels. To you. Because you have this relationship between you and your soul, remember?

That relationship is between you and you and when you from your physical human perspective think a thought, your soul knows which way you're pointing and what you're pointing at with that thought/perspective/belief/conclusion, and that gap or that space can only be felt by you as it relates to your desires, intentions and your soul's perspective.

**Let's be clear about something:** the point isn't that you find yourself in a situation that you're unhappy about, and your task is to go make yourself happy about it.

For instance, imagine you're at a buffet and you see a dish of turnips. You don't like turnips. Not one bit. Well, you don't have to force yourself to like them. You don't have to pretend you like them. You don't have to deny you don't like them. Just don't take the damn turnips. You can let the turnips be turnips, just don't put them on your plate. Instead, put the things you like to eat on your plate. Choose other things. You don't have to call the restaurant manager to scold him for putting turnips on the buffet, and you don't have to demand him to get them off the buffet. Just let them be.

This isn't about making yourself like something you don't like, or feel something you don't feel. As in the buffet example, there are plenty of other things to choose from. Trying to make yourself like something you've decided you don't like goes against your logic, and makes you dig-in and resist more. You get to have personal preferences, you get to have likes and dislikes. Just as you might prefer a Gala apple over a Granny Smith, or an orange over an apple. It doesn't make you wrong, bad, or unenlightened to prefer something. And sometimes, an asshole is just an asshole, but you don't have to keep making him wrong for being an asshole.

It is counter-productive to keep pointing out and pointing at, what you don't like and don't want on your plate. There's no need to amplify what you don't like any more than there's a need to get the turnips off the buffet before you can enjoy the rest of the food. There's no need to poke a bear, meaning — make it bigger. If you pay no attention to, let them be, and get on with the business of putting things on your plate that you want to eat, those turnips become a non-issue.

The same thing applies to this process of looking for the next good feeling. Doing this doesn't mean you have to feel good about something you've decided to feel bad about. It just means to find a better-feeling thought, either about the situation that you're associating with the "bad" feeling, or about something else entirely. Focus on something else.

If you've decided you don't like something someone is doing or saying, don't try to make yourself like it, but also, don't keep pointing it out. The more you point it out, the more you'll keep rendezvousing with more of it. And remember, that when you're angry at someone for being angry at you, it's like two chickens pecking at each other for being chickens. That's kind of unproductive and unhelpful, don't you think? You decide.

Just move on. Don't keep paying attention to it. Think about other things that feel good.

That's one of the ways to find the next best feeling.

Another misconception people have about this is that it's about completely changing how you feel, suddenly. Full stop from feeling crappy to happy. Not.

Imagine yourself standing on the edge of a 20-foot-wide stream, and I'm telling you to jump to the other side, which is 20 feet away.

You'd look at me and say, "Not happening any-time-soon, crazy lady. Nobody can jump that stream in one jump. It's 20 feet across."

So, then I'd ask you, "OK, if you want to get across and you mean to get across, how are you going to do it?" You, brilliant one, would look around us, see there's a bunch of stones in the area, and say, "I could lay some stones in place. By stepping on one stone at a time, incrementally-spaced, using each one to balance on before I step to the next one, I'd for sure make it across."

# Exactly.

To try to completely change your emotional state (how you feel) suddenly is like trying to jump the 20 foot stream. Try it, and you're likely to faceplant. You might try again, and again, and again, and fail again and again and again, and end up thinking you're not good at this. Then what inevitably comes out of a person's mouth who's tried jumping the 20 foot stream and failed time and again, is, "This shit doesn't work!"

# Not true. This shit does work. You've just got to do it with stepping stones.

Making the tiniest conceivable shift in your emotions by finding the next best feeling — whatever that is — is how you cross the stream. If that means going from being really angry to being slightly less angry, that's moving incrementally in the direction of your joy (and to the other side of that stream). That's stepping on the next little stepping stone, rather than trying to take the big leap.

If that means going from being really happy to being extra happy, that's moving in the direction of your joy, too.

It's the same concept.

It's not about making leaps from being unhappy to being happy. It's not faking-your-way-till-you-make-it into happy. It's about sticking with the journey. It's about taking the next step, and feeling the relief, the soothing, the desire to allow yourself to feel better. All those times you were trying to pretend you felt differently, all those times you tried to "jump the stream" and face-planted — it's just because you were trying to make a bigger leap than your current vibe would allow, rather than feeling your way across the stones that were there all along.

Finally, it's important for you to understand that this doesn't have to be hard. You don't have to "earn" your happy. We're also not "creating" happiness and good feelings out of nowhere. Your soul is constantly calling you toward your connection, toward happiness, toward wellbeing, and all the things you want. It's flowing continuously and effortlessly. Are you listening? Your soul never changes its frequency for you to feel it.

# YOU must adjust your frequency to feel it.

How much of that you're feeling and experiencing in your life is in direct relationship to your connection — how aligned you are, and/or how resistant you are. You can tell how close that alignment is by how you feel. When you're out of alignment, it's kind of like putting yourself in airplane mode. The tower is still broadcasting, you're just not receiving right now. You can easily switch into receiving mode again, all it takes is the push of a button — or a small shift in how you feel.

So change the subject.

Go to sleep.

Get outside.

Take a walk.

Pet your dog, cat, hamster, ferret, lizard or pet-of-choice.

Call a friend and talk about something else.

Distract yourself, choose a vibe that makes you feel better. You can always circle back to your bad-feeling if you find that you really miss it. (I won't judge.)

Whatever you do, don't double down on your resistance by digging in, focusing on it, or trying so-so-so hard to get out of it. And don't get mad at yourself for having resistance. Resistance is good. It lets you know where you're currently pointing. Know that you have total free-will to change your thoughts, your vibe, your perspective, and how you feel, which will make you a match to improvements, changes in your situation, and having more experiences along with the stuff you want. You can choose whether you want to exercise that right now. Or not.

If so, action, changes, and manifestations must follow suit with your vibe.

If not, recycling of what-is, changes to more of the same, and manifestations that don't feel good, will follow suit with your vibe.

It's as simple as that, and as unchangeable as the laws of gravity.

# Tune yourself differently, and everything changes.

But ... but ... but ... isn't this just a form of bypassing?

Absolutely not. Nope.

Bypassing is the choice to act as though something doesn't exist. Some people try to approach this process by completely stepping out of touch with reality, pretending that things aren't what they are.

That's like looking at the buffet, seeing those turnips you don't like, and then saying that turnips don't exist at all. That they've never been a vegetable. That there's no such thing as a root vegetable, or a turnip.

We're approaching this from an entirely different perspective: we acknowledge what is.

# Yep, there are those turnips.

We acknowledge how we feel about them: I really don't like those turnips. Yuck.

And then we choose what to do about it.

If you want to feel better, just leave the turnips to the side. You don't deny their existence, you merely don't give them your attention. In fact, you use their existence as information to choose where you do want to direct your attention.

This is about introducing more of the positive, not working to get rid of (or ignore) the negative.

So don't take something you've felt bad about for a long time, and try to shift it. Doing that is like trying to make your turnip into a Gala apple. Just let it be a turnip. We're not focusing on "digging out" all your traumas, or dramas. The easiest way to apply this is to, as best you can, think about more things you easily feel good about.

By thinking more things that feel good, by wanting to feel good and thinking about things that easily feel good, your vibe changes and acclimates to what's now the theme or essence of your thoughts. Any shift in your vibe to the positive affects every area of your life.

You can't keep reintroducing the thoughts that feel bad and expect to feel better. You can't keep reintroducing the thoughts that feel bad and expect things to change for the better. That would be like regurgitating your food and expecting it would taste good. Not likely. You're not a cow, so stop it.

# When you make a positive shift in how you feel, you're making way for tangible, positive changes.

Do more things that make you feel good, and experience your life changing easily, without effort.

# step 4:

## Keep doing that.

That's it. That's the steps: practice awareness. Own your vibe. Find the next best feeling. Keep doing that. Simple.

Because you're a smartypants, you might think it needs to be more complicated. Or you might try to complicate it. Don't. It's not about suffering and struggling your way towards happiness, enlightenment, or anything. It's also not just about eating bonbons on the couch, thinking the occasional positive thought and expecting the world to fall at your feet. Ta-da!

It's about intentional, consistent, frequent awareness, ownership, and shifts toward your satisfaction, your happiness, fulfillment and joy. It's vibrational movements that you feel. It's cause and effect.

"But Christine, a magical genie didn't come out and fix everything overnight!"

Right.

This is not about magic, there's no fairy wand to wave. It's about you creating you, and you creating your life. And you have habits, beliefs, expectations, a life you've lived, that's all a part of you.

You're not being asked to erase it, make it go away, get a personality transplant or a lobotomy.

Tuning in to your connection, your soul, which also means tuning into your desire to feel good, moving in the direction of it, and letting that train your thoughts, beliefs, and expectations into new territory that aligns more with who you-really-are, changes everything. Again, it's cause and effect. It's something that you practice until it becomes a habit. It's something that you show yourself, works. If you throw a tennis ball for your dog often enough, that dog's consistently, reliably, going to run after the ball and bring it back to you.

You may not find yourself taking different actions, or changing anything tangible in your life, externally, at first, but if you apply this and practice it, you're going to feel better. You're going to notice where you have the tendency to focus more on the negative side of things than the positive side of things. And you can change that.

You've been in the driver's seat all along. Now you know it.

It's significant to understand that there's likely some momentum in-place. You've been thinking and feeling and thinking and feeling in habitual ways perhaps for a while now, which has created a certain flow of energy.

But here's the great thing: it stops when you think other thoughts. Easy as that.

If you put just a little less attention on the things that feel bad, and a little more attention on the things that feel good or better, the momentum of the unwanted naturally becomes less.

Picture two fire pits, equally burning. The one on the left is your "negative" thoughts and feelings, and the one on the right is your desired thoughts and feelings (the ones that feel better to you). Once you decide you want to feel better, you've taken a step toward adding fewer sticks to the left-side fire pit. If you add only the occasional stick to the fire pit on the left and intentionally add more sticks to the fire pit on the right, eventually, the one on the left is going to go out, and the one on the right is going to burn better.

It's not that you're getting rid of the fire on the left by doing something. It's just going to stop burning because of your lack of attention and tending to it. In giving less attention to the one, you're giving more attention to the other. It's that easy.

It can take time, and it doesn't always feel easy, because of that momentum, but if you substitute something you've been thinking or doing, with something else, soon what-was won't be, because you've replaced it with something else. It's about replacing an old habit by forming a new one.

You'll still do things, think, perceive and feel things out of habit — like how you habitually turn on the light switch, even when you know your power's out — but eventually, you'll stop because your new habits will have replaced your old ones.

# That's why you need to be steady when it comes to this work. Mastery isn't about perfection, it's about understanding that mastery is never done.

It takes consistency. It takes the intention to step on the stone to cross the stream, and then move to the next stone, or if you can't move to the next stone, hang out for awhile, with the intention to keep heading across at some point. If you keep going back to the other side though, or if you try to jump too far, you'll face-plant and you'll believe "this shit" doesn't work for you. Or that you're not good at it. When, in fact, it IS working perfectly and you can get "good at it." You can go to the "bad-feeling" side of the stream, and things will play out in your life that match how you feel. You're still demonstrating your power either way. It's just whether you want to feel better or worse.

You have to care enough about how you feel and want to feel good to think the thought that feels better, or change the subject to one that does. Consider this your new approach to being, not just something you do every now and again. Think of this as a lifestyle change vs. a fad that will eventually fade.

Things are going to happen and trigger you, and you're going to feel bad. Embrace all your emotions, because they're all good. They're all helpful information. They're all feedback to empower yourself.

Things are going to happen that you might not have seen coming (wanted or not), as if they "came out of the blue." You know differently now.

Your capacity
to feel good
is limitless.
And so is your
capacity to feel
bad. Which
way you go is
up to you.

This is just
the beginning.

## The key to living a good life is feeling good.

A happy life is nothing but a series of choices to feel good.

Everything you want is for that purpose. If you start making the correlation between your thoughts and how you feel, and how that affects your life, and if you have the desire to feel the best that you can, your life will progressively and endlessly continue to become what you want it to be.

The key is feeling good along the way. Not "when." Not "if." Not "as long as." Just because.

This truly is just the beginning. You can apply this knowledge to any part of your life, any subject, any time, anywhere, no matter what. You are now aware that you're in control, you are now aware of your power to create, and you have the tools to apply it, and to let it be easy.

So enjoy this process. If you discover something here that works for you, live it, be it.

If others around you notice and want to learn where your mojo is coming from, then you can tell them. But unless they're asking, it's often better to keep it to yourself. Otherwise, you're going to be that jerk know-it-all who's discovered the secret to the universe and has to tell everybody. Let people discover it in their own time, at their own pace. Just live it in the best way you possibly can, for yourself.

Now go. Live your life.

Get what you want.

Create what you desire.

Know you're worthy.

And enjoy the ride. Because
that's what it's always all about.

I'm excited for what you're in
the process of discovering.

# THANK YOU

To my husband, Jack and my daughter, Franki — you are my everything.

........................................

To my friend and editor, Rachel Allen, my book designer,
Sutton Long, and to Christine Kloser for getting me started in a real way.
You are all incredible and talented humans.

........................................

To the authors, speakers, teachers and leaders that I've learned from,
including and not limited to: Florence Scovel Shinn, Walter Wattles,
Napoleon Hill, Abraham-Hicks, Neil Donald Walsch, Yanla Vanzant, Earl
Nightingale, Richard Bach, Gary Zukav, Alanis Morissette, and Debbie Ford.

........................................

To my parents, Phil and Gerri Moore and Hélène and Kem Hür.
You formed and informed me in so many valuable ways. I love you.
To my in-laws, Audrey and John Meyer, you've been a
blessing right from the start.

........................................

To Josh Greenbaum, Katie MacDonald, Ronell Martz, Zach Hoesly,
Gabriela Effron, Adam Rockefeller Growald, Lisa VanderVeen, Sabina
King, Nikki Groom, Kym McNicholas, Kate Ayala, Jodi Coleman, Jennifer
Copeland, Amber Cleveland-Lewter, Beth Bennati, Lanie Gabbard, Andi
Tinker, Peter Mackey, and so many more — my clients, my friends, my
colleagues. For providing me with opportunities to do the work that I love
and for your generosity, friendship, feedback and encouragement.

........................................

To Austin Kleon for inspiring me to create this book.

........................................

To all of you who are reading this book and spreading the message.

........................................

I appreciate you.

Christine Meyer is a life coach who believes people are more powerful than they realize. Since 2002, she's skillfully guided philanthropists, investors, entrepreneurs, media personalities, thought leaders, and other coaches toward the conscious and deliberate creation of the lives they want through the mastery of their alignment. As a sought-after speaker, founding member and regular contributor to the Forbes Coaches Council, she's excited to share the fundamental foundations offered to her private clients in her first book, *Keep It Simple, Smartypants!* Find her online at christinemeyercoaching.com.

Peter Mackey @mackeyphoto